Hearing

Lillian Wright

RSVP

RAINTREE
STECK-VAUGHN
PUBLISHERS

The Steck-Vaughn Company

Austin, Texas

Series Editor: Pippa Pollard
Science Editor: Kim Merlino
Design: Sally Boothroyd
Project Manager: Julie Klaus
Electronic Production:
   Scott Melcer
Artwork: Mainline Design
Cover Art: Mainline Design

Library of Congress
Cataloging-in-Publication Data
Wright, Lillian.
     Hearing / Lillian Wright.
        p.   cm. — (First starts)
     Includes index.
     ISBN 0-8114-5516-5
     1. Hearing — Juvenile literature.
[1. Hearing. 2. Senses and
sensation.]   I. Title.   II. Series.
QP462.2.W75 1995
612.8'5—dc20   94-10719
                              CIP AC
Printed and bound in the
United States

1 2 3 4 5 6 7 8 9 0 LB 98 97 96 95 94

Contents

What Is Hearing?

We are able to hear many sounds if our ears are working properly. We can hear very soft sounds, like a fly buzzing. We can hear very loud sounds, like an airplane flying overhead. When we listen, we can discover things about the world around us. Listening can tell us about things we may not be able to see.

▽ Hearing is one of our five senses.

Looking at Our Ears

We have two ears, one on each side of our head, which we use to detect sounds. Only the soft, outer part of the ear can be seen. The rest is protected by our bony skull because it is very delicate. Sounds are made by air **vibrating**, or moving back and forth.

▷ Our ears let us hear someone else talking.

▽ Sound waves cannot be seen, but travel through the air to our ears.

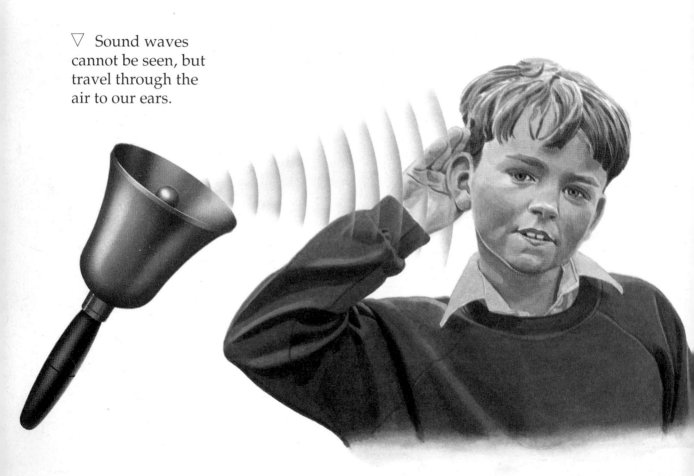

Our Ears Are Different

Our ears vary in shape and size. The shape of our ears is inherited. This means they are like our parents' ears. Some people have large lobes at the bottom of their ears. Others have none at all. Some people can wiggle their outer ears. Most humans cannot move their ears, though. Many animals can.

▷ Rabbits have long ears at the top of their heads, which they can move in the direction the sound is coming from.

▽ Our ears come in all shapes and sizes.

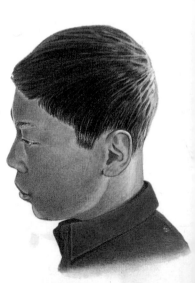

How Do We Hear?

The outer part of our ears is used to "catch" sounds. Sounds usually reach our ears by traveling through the air as sound waves. Sound waves move along the ear canal to the **eardrum**. This vibrates and makes the middle ear and the inner ear vibrate. Messages travel to the brain along the **auditory nerve**. Our brain tells us what we are hearing.

▽ Sounds "beat" our eardrums like a musician playing a drum.

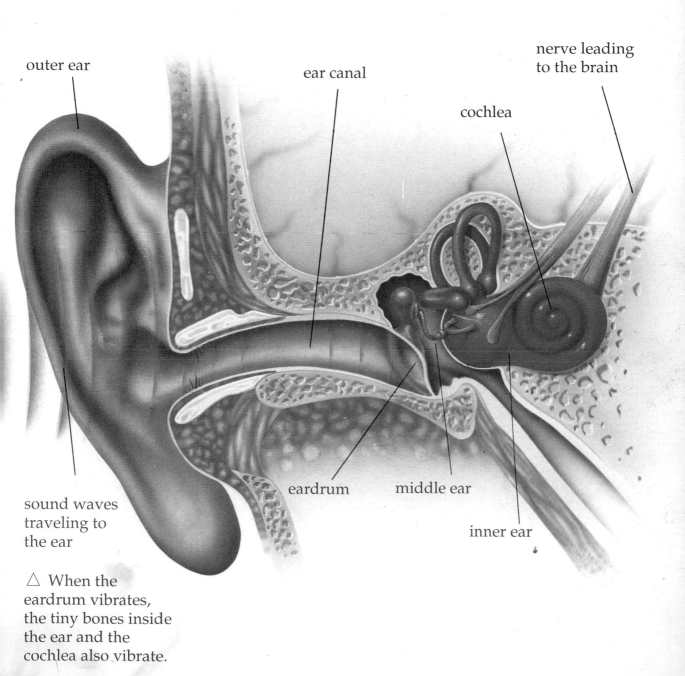

outer ear

ear canal

nerve leading
to the brain

cochlea

sound waves
traveling to
the ear

eardrum

middle ear

inner ear

△ When the
eardrum vibrates,
the tiny bones inside
the ear and the
cochlea also vibrate.

Hearing Sounds

Sounds travel through the air at about 1,116 feet (340 m) every second. Quiet sounds travel just as quickly as loud sounds. But quiet sounds do not go as far. Sounds can travel faster through liquids like water and solids like wood or metal than they do through the air. To hear all the sounds being made around us, the sound waves have to reach our eardrum and make it vibrate.

▷ The sound of the referee's voice or whistle travels through the air to the ears of soccer players.

▽ The tapping sound is louder when the child has his ear on the desk. This is because sound travels better through a solid than through the air.

Listening Carefully

Our ears can hear loud and soft sounds. Sometimes we have to move closer to a very soft sound to hear it. A doctor may use a **stethoscope** so that he or she can hear our breathing or heartbeat. Some sounds are so loud that our ears can hear them even when we are far away. Many animals can hear sounds that we cannot.

▽   A whale can hear very low sounds over hundreds of miles.

▷ A bat can hear
very high sounds.

▽ A doctor
can hear a quiet
heartbeat, using a
special instrument
called a stethoscope.

How Well Can You Hear?

Some people can hear better than others. But this is not because they have better ears. They may listen more carefully. A doctor or nurse checks children at school, in case they have something wrong with their ears. Someone may be able to hear better with one ear than with the other. Some people can hear high sounds better than low ones. Soft sounds may be difficult to hear.

▷ People called audiologists can check to see if we can hear high and low sounds properly, using special machines.

◁ We whisper when we don't want others to hear us.

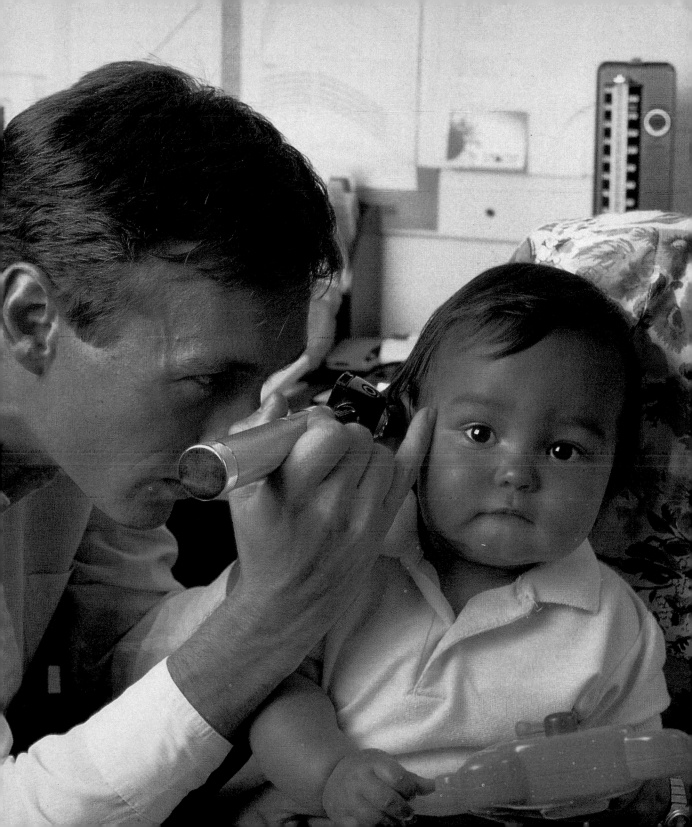

Recognizing Sounds

Sometimes we can hear soft sounds that we know very well, like our own name being called. We learn to recognize many sounds, even if they reach our ears at the same time. If there are a lot of sounds around us, we may not be able to hear what we want. If we are not listening, the sounds may reach our ears, but they are not "heard" by our brain.

▷ We usually hear our own name being called.

▷ Sometimes we don't want to hear the sounds that reach our ears!

▷ On the telephone
we may not always
recognize who is
speaking.

Why Have Two Ears?

Our two ears are at either side of our head to let us hear sounds from all around. If we hear someone calling for help, we know which way to run to get to them. Animals that have their ears at the front of the head can move the outer ears around. This lets them know exactly where any sound is coming from.

▽ If we cannot see where a sound is coming from, our two ears will tell us.

▷ This child's ear that is nearest the window will hear the other person's voice calling first.

▽ Listening for sounds of danger is important for a deer's survival.

Ear Care

We need to look after our ears so that we can hear clearly. We need to wash the outer ears as well. We must not put anything inside our ears. That could damage the ears or prevent us from hearing properly. Even loud noises can hurt or damage our ears.

▷ People who work with noisy machines wear hearing protectors, or ear defenders. These protect their ears from very loud sounds.

◁ Sticky yellow wax in the outer ear and ear canal traps dirt and dust and keeps them from entering our ears.

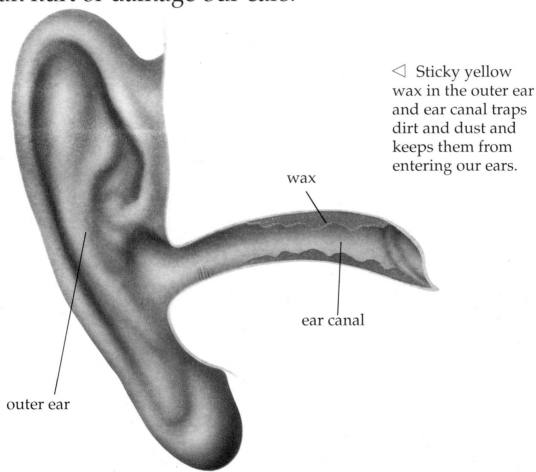

wax

ear canal

outer ear

Hearing Loss

Some people cannot hear clearly. This may be because of an accident or illness. Some babies are born with some degree of hearing loss or damage. **Hearing aids** can help some of these people to hear more. People who are hearing impaired use their hands to "talk." This is called **signing**. Some learn to tell what others are saying by watching their lips.

▽ Hearing aids are usually electronic devices that are designed to pick up sounds and make them louder.

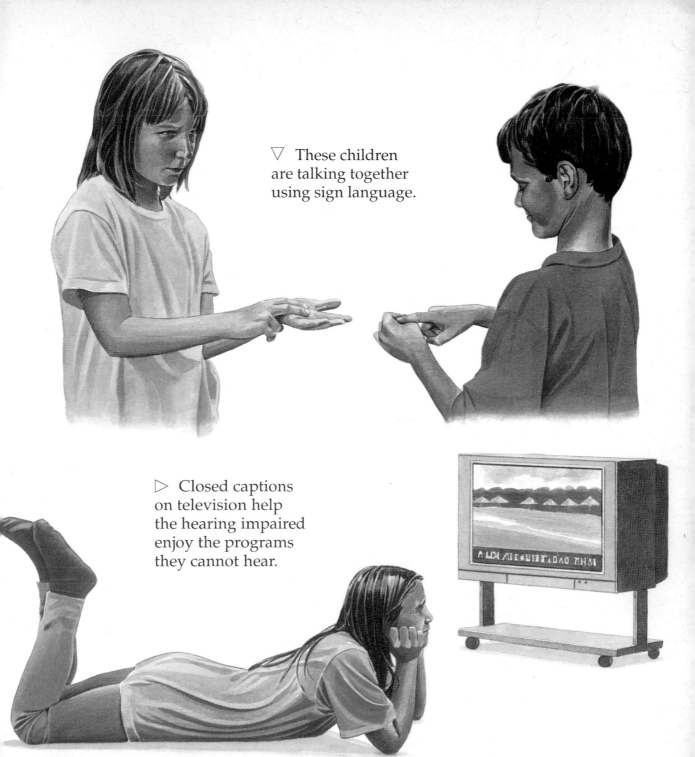

▽ These children
are talking together
using sign language.

▷ Closed captions
on television help
the hearing impaired
enjoy the programs
they cannot hear.

Enjoying Listening

Besides loud and soft sounds, we can hear high and low sounds. Musical instruments can make all sorts of different sounds—the beat of a drum or the toot of a trumpet. Music is a mix of sounds that we can enjoy. Most people around the world listen to songs and music. They can be recorded on cassette tapes or compact disks for everybody to enjoy.

▷ We can recognize many different musical instruments playing at the same time, such as in an orchestra.

▽ Tape recorders, radios, and televisions let us listen to all kinds of sounds and music.

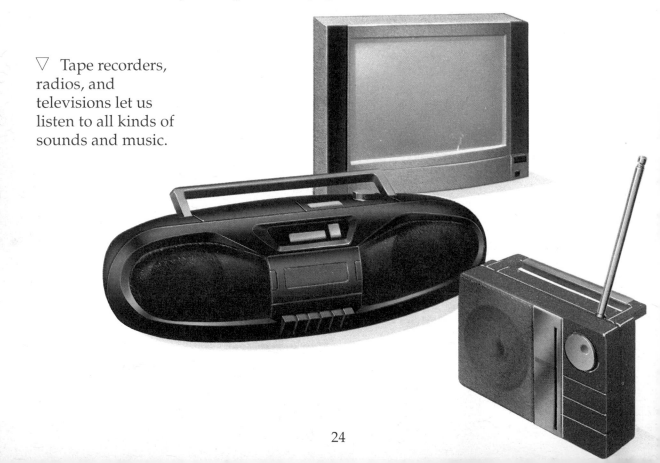

Noise Pollution

Sounds that we do not want to listen to can be very annoying. Many machines that we use make noises that we do not want. Airplanes and cars help us to travel, but they are very noisy. All unwanted noise is called noise pollution. Some machines can be made quieter.

▷ Life in cities is usually very noisy. Count all the noisemakers you see in this picture.

▷ The muffler on this motorcycle helps to cut down noise.

Hearing from Far Away

If we want to hear something better, we can go closer to the source of the sound. Sometimes it is not possible to do this, and so machines have been invented to help us. A **megaphone** makes the voice sound louder at a distance. Radios and telephones are inventions that send and receive voice messages over very long distances. **Echoes** are another way that we hear from far away.

▷ Telephones allow us to speak to people thousands of miles away.

▷ The sound of a loud call travels back from the cliff face in an echo.

Things to Do

- Tap a tabletop with your finger.
  Then listen again with your ear on
  the tabletop. What do you notice?

- Collect as many pictures of animal
  ears as possible. Compare them
  with your own ears.

- Think about how you can help
  to reduce noise pollution. Do you
  always listen to very loud music?
  Do you really need to?

Useful Addresses:

National Association of the Deaf
814 Thayer Avenue
Silver Springs, MD 20910

Deaf Reach
3521 12th Street NE
Washington, DC 20017

Alexander Graham Bell
  Association for the Deaf
3417 Volta Place NW
Washington, DC 20007

American Speech-Language
  and Hearing Association
10801 Rockville Pike
Rockville, MD 20852

Glossary

auditory nerve The nerve that goes from the ear to the brain.

cochlea The coiled tube inside the ear that converts sound waves into electrical signals that pass along the auditory nerve to the brain.

eardrum The thin, skinlike layer that is stretched across the entrance to the middle ear. It vibrates when sound waves hit it.

echo A repeated sound. An echo is heard when a sound bounces back from a distant hill or wall so that you hear it again.

hearing aid A device to make sounds louder and help those who are hearing impaired to hear better.

megaphone A funnel-shaped instrument used to make a voice louder.

signing Movements of the hands that stand for words and ideas and form a language that people who cannot hear well can use.

stethoscope An instrument used to hear sounds produced in the lungs, heart, or other parts of the body.

vibrating Moving rapidly back and forth.

31

Index

Photographic credits:
Action-Plus Photographic 11; Chris Fairclough Colour Library 7, 25; Eye Ubiquitous (David Cumming) 27, (T. Nottingham) 19, (Paul Sohoult) 3; Sally and Richard Greenhill 21; Science Photo Library (Damien Lovegrove) 13, 15; Spectrum Colour Library 8, 17, 22, 29.

© 1994 Watts Books